CON

Acknowledgements

The author wishes to thank Aelred Stubbs and Donald Woods, both of whose books have made Steve Biko and his work more widely known; Barney Pityana for reading before publication this account of the rise of Black Consciousness (although any mistakes are mine not his); Sue Twiselton for seeing this through to publication and for picture research; and Kate Thomlinson and Louise Basson who read a first draft. Further, to my wife, Mary, for all her help.

The author and publisher would like to thank the following for permission to reproduce photographs:
IDAF cover, 6, 9, 13, 15, 21, 29, 31, 33, 34, 37, 41, 42, 43, 48, 51, 54, 56–57, 62–63, 65, 69, 71, 73, 81, 83, 85, 88, 90; Pixfeatures 38–39; Popperfoto 22, 24, 79

RACIAL TERMS

The words used to describe South Africa's different race groups are often confusing. The government classifies people into four categories: white, black, Coloured and Indian. However, to many in South Africa these classifications are unacceptable. Here is a simple guideline to the use of racial terminology in this book:

African: The indigenous people of Africa.

Afrikaner: Descendants of the first white settlers (mainly of Dutch origin), who govern the country today.

Bantu: This has been used by the South African government to refer to Africans. It means 'people'. In this book, it is only used when quoting a specific law or government department (e.g. Bantu Administration Department).

Black: All those who are at the receiving end of apartheid: Africans, Coloureds and Indians (unless used in a direct quote where the official term means African).

Coloured: People of mixed race. (This term is used in the official sense, as unfortunately there is no alternative in common use.)

Indian: People whose ancestors came from the Indian subcontinent. (Official use and accepted by most South Africans.)

Native: Term first used in South Africa to describe Africans. In this book, it is used when quoting an individual or referring to a specific institution, law or government department (e.g. Natives' Land Act).

Non-white: The Black Consciousness movement rejected this term, which was used by some South Africans to describe those who are not white. In this book, the term is only used when referring to this subject.

White: People who come from, or whose ancestors came from, a European country.

Steve Biko: hopes for a peaceful end to apartheid died with him.

1
INTRODUCTION

❝ You are either alive and proud or you are dead, and when you are dead you don't care anyway. And your method of death can itself be a politicising thing .... ❞

These are the words of Stephen Biko, a young black leader in South Africa fighting the system of government known as apartheid. They are taken from an interview with an American journalist in 1977. Soon after, Biko was arrested by the South African security police. He was held in solitary confinement, interrogated and beaten. Less than a month after his arrest he was dead.

Steve Biko's death led to a worldwide outcry. Political detainees had died before and have since. But to many people, inside and outside South Africa, the hopes for a peaceful end to apartheid died with Biko. Five weeks after his death the organisations opposing apartheid which Biko had helped to establish were all made illegal by the South African government.

They were not the first: two black organisations – the African National Congress (ANC) and the Pan-African-ist Congress (PAC) – had been banned in 1961. Nor were they the last. More recently, in February 1988, a total of 17 other organisations which were working against apartheid were also banned from carrying out any activity that the government thought was political. The South

African government has also declared a state of emergency, which gives it even greater powers to crack down on those whom it regards as a threat. Most public meetings are illegal, newspapers and television cannot report many protests against the government, and the 'security forces' – usually the police or army – can arrest people without a warrant and hold them in detention for unlimited periods. Nobody, apart from the police, is allowed to see detainees without permission: not parents, relatives, the family doctor or the family lawyer. In the case of Steve Biko, and for at least seventy others, this system of detention without trial has meant death. In most cases, family and friends of the detainees believe that the security police, through torture and neglect, have been responsible.

All those who have died in detention have a common link: they have actively opposed apartheid. But what is this system which arouses such strong feelings, within South Africa and in the world beyond?

Apartheid is a word coined by white South Africans who speak Afrikaans. (Afrikaans, which comes from the Dutch language, is used by the descendants of the first white settlers in South Africa. These Afrikaners, as they are called, rule the country today.) Apartheid means, literally, 'apartness'. It is used, almost as a shorthand term, to describe the policy of trying to keep white and black South Africans separate from one another. Opponents of apartheid say that the system is also meant to keep white people in control of the country. When apartheid became a 'dirty word' internationally, South Africa's rulers changed it to 'separate development' instead. The policy has also euphemistically been called 'parallel development' and is now sometimes known as 'co-operative co-existence'.

One face of apartheid: park benches forbidden to blacks
– even nannies.

Apartheid's bad reputation originally stemmed from the way the system was introduced. The South African government did not consult black people about everybody being kept separate. It simply said: whites will live here and blacks cannot; whites can do these jobs and blacks cannot; whites can go to school and university here and blacks cannot; whites can use these hospitals, hotels, parks, playgrounds, beaches, sportsfields, swimming baths, toilets, buses and trains – even cemeteries – and blacks cannot. And laws were passed to enforce apartheid, with penalties for those who did not comply, ranging from corporal punishment and fines to five years imprisonment. The government tried to keep people of different races separate in every possible way. The system was structured so that white people benefited most from it.

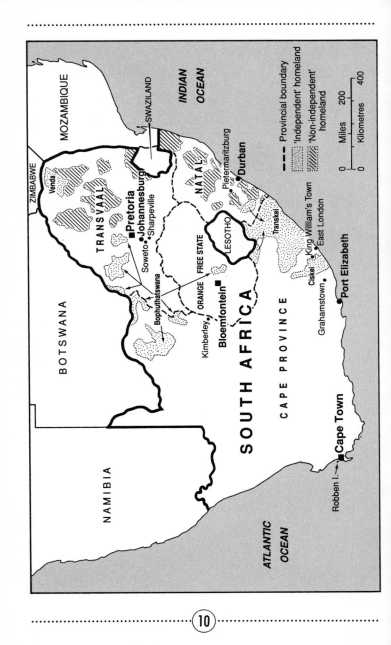

Apartheid came to be official government policy when the National Party* won the 1948 general election. Before then, there had been some segregation of different races and blacks were generally poorer than whites. After 1948, the National Party passed laws to make sure that whites stayed on top. For example, everybody had to be registered at birth according to race. That classification determined one's entire life. As time went on, more laws were passed by parliament making apartheid even tighter. The pass laws were made more rigid in an attempt to control the movement of Africans, and the homelands policy relocated many to areas which the government decided were African 'tribal' homes. Coloureds and Africans lost what voice they had in parliament. Instead they were given other bodies with little power through which they were supposed to speak.

Into this situation in the late 1960s – the ANC and PAC banned and many of its supporters in jail, millions of people uprooted from their homes for political reasons and a general air of black despair – came Steve Biko and his ideas of Black Consciousness*.

* See glossary

2
GROWING UP

❛ My friendships, my love, my education, my thinking and every other facet of my life have been carved and shaped within the context of separate development . . . ❜

Steve Biko, September 1970

Steve Biko was born on 18 December 1946, 17 months before the National Party came to power and introduced apartheid. He was one of four children with a brother and two sisters. His father, who died when Biko was four, worked as a clerk and his mother was a domestic servant for white families in and around King William's Town, a small, rather sleepy place in the south-east corner of South Africa. 'King', as the town is commonly known, is the centre of what later became the 'independent' homeland of Ciskei. The Biko household, according to one of Steve's later political colleagues, Barney Pityana, was a truly extended family:

'They all learned to share and, according to their capacities, made contributions to family life. This left a lasting impression on Steve. He was brought up not just with his brother and sisters, for his mother, while she was in full-time employment, also brought up children of relatives. Steve was impressed by his mother's philosophical attitude to the daily struggle to make ends meet and her total commitment to offer what help she could, not only to her own children but to those who called upon her in times of need ... It was the seed from which a political system [Black Consciousness] grew that was to change the face of South African politics.'

In the years after 1948, critics say that the policy of apartheid or 'separate development' meant more separation than development. While the young Biko was growing up, there were few factories or businesses to provide jobs: clerical work for men and domestic service for women were fairly typical forms of employment among many Africans in King. Outside the town, Africans had smallholdings or worked on white farms — usually for desperately poor wages.

At the time of Biko's birth, there was strict social segregation between black and white. Africans lived in separate 'locations' (now called townships) on the

Apartheid in the 1950s: the poverty-stricken township of Alexandra near Johannesburg. Today it is surrounded by expensive white suburbs.

outskirts of white cities and towns. Schools were segregated. African political thought was supposed to be channelled through the Native Representative Council. This was a body of 12 elected and four nominated members (and white officials) who passed resolutions that were almost totally ignored by the government of the day: it was, in the words of one of its members, a 'toy telephone'.

From 1948, new laws reinforced the policy of apartheid. The Prohibition of Mixed Marriages Act of 1949 did exactly what its name suggests. An amendment to the Immorality Act in 1950 banned sexual relationships between whites and any other race group. The 1950 Population Registration Act, one of the 'pillars of apartheid', classified everybody into one of four races: white, black, Coloured, and Indian. The Group Areas Act of 1950 completed earlier apartheid laws. It allowed the government to make living and working areas totally segregated, and to stop people of one race group owning property in an area reserved for another. By 1985 a total of 126,176 families had been moved from their homes under this Act: 66% were Coloured, 32% Indian, and 2% white. By 1988 over 83% of the group areas proclaimed were for whites only.

Most of these laws affected Coloureds and Indians more than Africans who had long been forced to live further away from whites. But from 1951 the policy of apartheid began to concentrate on Africans. The Bantu Education Act of 1953 took control of African education away from state-aided mission schools to the Department of Native Affairs in central government. The then-minister and later Prime Minister was Hendrik Verwoerd, the chief architect of apartheid. Notoriously, he said when introducing 'Bantu Education': 'If the native in South Africa today in any kind of school in existence is being taught to expect that he will live his adult life under a policy of equal rights, he is making a big mistake ... There is no place for him in the European community above the level of certain forms of labour ...'

Spending on African education was (and is) far below that for whites: in 1953, for example, just under £9 was spent on each African pupil and approximately £64 on each white pupil. By 1985–6 the figure was just over seven times as much for whites as for Africans. African schools suffered from poor facilities, under-qualified and badly-paid teachers, as well as a poor pupil-teacher ratio: 41.6 pupils per teacher in African schools as opposed to 15.7 per teacher in white schools. Teachers often had to take two classes a day or one teacher would be expected to be in charge of two classes in the same room. There was a high drop-out rate among students: only 1.8% of African pupils reached the final year of schooling compared with 6.5% of whites in 1985. In the same year it

'Bantu Education': African children 'fobbed off' with inferior schooling.

was calculated that 49.5% of Africans left school after four years or less and were therefore semi-literate or illiterate.

In 1966 the British educationalist, Dr Robert Birley, visited four secondary schools in Soweto, the black township outside Johannesburg where nearly 2500 children were being taught science. 'Between them they have 13 Bunsen burners, six balances (and one more which seemed to me quite useless), and three microscopes. A school of about 1000 children receives an annual grant for scientific equipment of about R35 [then about £18] a year out of which it has to buy the essential materials for the very simplest chemical experiments.'

The quality of 'Bantu Education' was a highly-charged political issue throughout Biko's school career and beyond. Many of those subjected to it thought that they were being fobbed off with inferior schooling. In recent years, spending on African education has increased dramatically as the government realised that the economy needed better-educated Africans, among other reasons. But critics argue that more is still being spent on white pupils and that the gap between the two has not narrowed significantly. Further, the demand by African pupils and their elders has not been merely for increased finances. It has been for one department of education to control all schools, rather than a separate department for Africans which perpetuates apartheid and inferior education.

Biko had a better education than most African children. He attended one of the most famous African schools, Lovedale Institute, but was expelled with many other boys – including Barney Pityana – after a strike in 1963. (School strikes have been common in black schools, often over the quality of food, corporal punishment, and poor teaching.) Biko then went to Marianhill in Natal, a Roman Catholic school, before enrolling at the University of Natal in Durban in 1966 to study medicine.

Biko's achievement of a place at university was unusual: in 1965 only 323 Africans were granted a university entrance pass in their final year of schooling while the total African school enrolment for that year was more than 1.6 million. In 1966 he was one of 2926 Africans at university out of a total student enrolment of almost 65,000.

Nearly all of those who were attending university every day were at the so-called 'tribal colleges'. These were universities specially established, under the policy of apartheid, for different tribes or races. Facilities were usually poor and the professors and lecturers often said to be second rate. These colleges included University College of the Western Cape for Coloureds, Westville for Indians, and Zululand for Zulus. Biko's university, Natal, was supposedly multiracial. But of the 5000 students at the university, just over 11% were black.

More recently, the policy of strict university apartheid has been watered down and today there are more black students at the 'white' English-language universities than ever before: about 20% in 1986. The number of African students at all the country's universities has also increased dramatically: from the 2926 when Biko first enrolled to about 60,000 today. So, too, has the number of Coloured students – up to nearly 14,000 from less than 1300 – and Indians: 18,400 compared to 3100.

It was while Biko was at the University of Natal's medical school that politics emerged as his main interest. And it was then that the philosophy of Black Consciousness was first formed.

3
A HISTORY OF OPPRESSION

> ❝ ... blacks are suffering from an inferiority complex – a result of 300 years of deliberate oppression, denigration and derision ... ❞
>
> Steve Biko, August 1970

Biko's analysis of South African history is not one that appeals to many whites. The simplistic white view is that Europeans and Africans arrived in southern Africa at roughly the same time, in the middle of the 17th century. Whites argue that this justifies the 'homelands' policy separating the country into white and black, as nobody can claim prior ownership. (Some extreme rightwing Afrikaners even plan a 'homeland' for Coloureds.) Many also maintain that the first white settlers (mainly Dutch and called Boers at the time) spread throughout the country bringing 'civilisation' to the Africans who were divided by tribal wars, and that the country was later developed economically, largely by British capital, after the discovery of diamonds and gold.

The Black Consciousness interpretation is rather different. 'Whereas the African culture was unsophisticated and simple,' Biko wrote in 1971, 'the Anglo-Boer culture had all the trappings of a colonialist culture and therefore was heavily equipped for conquest. Where they could, they conquered by persuasion, using a highly exclusive religion that denounced all other gods and demanded a strict code of behaviour with respect to clothing, education, ritual, and custom. Where it was impossible to convert, firearms were readily available and used to advantage. Hence the Anglo-Boer culture was the more powerful culture in almost all facets. This is where the African began to lose a grip on himself and his surroundings.'

South African history can be heavily weighted to one side or another through political bias. Many history books used in schools and universities are partial, setting out the government's view of South African history. In the past few years, however, historians have been writing books that take the African point of view and experience into account. An important element of Biko's philosophy of Black Consciousness was an attempt to correct the one-sided history that he — and most South Africans — had been taught. And some knowledge of South African history is needed to understand both apartheid and Steve Biko's life and work.

*

Europeans settled in what is now Cape Town in 1652. These settlers worked for the Dutch East India Company and their purpose was to provide fresh food for Dutch ships trading with the Far East: there was no plan to colonise southern Africa. But the Dutch East India Company found that people working for themselves were more efficient than company servants. These 'free burghers' (free citizens) began to grow food needed for passing ships from 1657. White stock farmers in search of new grazing later moved north and east from Cape Town. After the mid-18th century they encountered Africans in large numbers who were also competing for land.

Africans had inhabited the north of present-day South Africa by the 5th century A.D. In the 18th century population growth, political instability, and economic opportunity had encouraged them to move south, while Europeans were moving north and east. The two met in the eastern corner of South Africa: what is today the eastern part of Cape Province.

The two cultures could hardly have been more different. The Boers were rugged individualists, slave-owners, cut off from much of the European Enlightenment* (the 'Age of Reason') of the time, strongly religious but casting themselves in the role of a chosen people and black non-Christians as 'damned barbarians'. In contrast, African culture was, in Biko's words, 'a community-based' society, where religion was 'manifest in our daily lives', where 'poverty was a foreign concept', where all worked together and there was 'no such thing as individual land ownership'.

These two groups clashed towards the end of the 18th century. Soon afterwards control of the Cape began to pass to the British who first occupied it in 1795 after France invaded the Netherlands. They took formal possession in 1814–15 as part of the Napoleonic Wars* settlements. A few years later London decided that the best way to keep the peace on the troubled Eastern Cape frontier was to import large numbers of new migrants from Britain. In 1820 about 5000 Britons were brought to farm around Grahamstown. These migrants would, in effect, form a human wall of settlements that would make it more difficult for Africans to 'invade' the Cape.

The 1820 Settlers brought some elements of enlightened thinking which were to lead to a more liberal approach to the running of the Cape. Government efficiency improved; pass laws introduced by the Dutch to

Slave labour: Cape farmers used slaves until abolition in 1834.

control black workers were repealed; equality before the law between black and white was established in 1828; and slavery was abolished in 1834. The British tried to replace the Dutch language with English and British missionaries criticised the Boers' treatment of blacks. The Boers were not impressed by any of this. A new war between Africans and whites broke out.

The Boers reacted by leaving the Cape in the 'Great Trek' of 1836–7. They went first to Natal, only to leave in 1842 after the British annexed the territory. The Boers' next refuges were what later became the Orange Free State and Transvaal (then called the South African Republic). The Boer republics, established in the mid-19th century, deprived Africans of land. Sometimes this was implemented by the whites signing treaties with African chiefs who, in fact, had no power to do so.

The Boers travelled hundreds of miles by ox wagon during the Great Trek.

African society, as Biko has pointed out, regarded the land as belonging to the people: chiefs had no right to sell it off. The Boer republics also established the principle of 'no equality [between the races] in church or state'. For example, in some churches blacks were not allowed to attend services. This principle was, many believe, the basis for apartheid laws a century later.

In the Cape that the 6000 Trekkers had left, political theory was geared towards the ideal of gradual integration and equality. The vote was granted to people 'without distinction to class or colour' but with property qualifications. Later, however, the qualifications were raised to keep out 'unwesternised peasants'. In Natal, the franchise* was also supposed to be non-racial. But a devious law was passed depriving all blacks of their right to vote, apart from a couple of hundred Africans and Indians. (The Indians had been imported to work on the sugar plantations.)

The four states – the Cape, Natal, South African Republic, and Orange Free State – lived side by side with some uneasiness for years. When diamonds were discovered at Kimberley in 1870 the situation changed quite radically. Money and people from abroad poured into the area. Africans, too, joined the diamond rush, to earn money and provided the hard labour force enabling railway lines to be built. In 1886 gold was discovered on the Witwatersrand and the city of Johannesburg sprung up almost overnight. Again, it was the Africans who provided the physical labour, often working under very poor conditions.

Gold and diamonds pushed the four states away from a mainly agricultural economy towards a more urban economy based largely on mining. It also led to the British (under imperialists like Cecil Rhodes) extending their influence and, at the turn of the century, to the Anglo-Boer War. This resulted in defeat for the two Boer republics. Less than ten years later, in 1910, the Union of South Africa was established. Its leaders for the next forty years were to be the very generals who had led the fight against the British: Louis Botha, Barry Hertzog, and Jan Christian Smuts.

Not everyone was happy about the new Union. Right-wing Afrikaners regarded the first premier, Louis Botha, and Jan Christian Smuts who succeeded him in 1919, as willing tools of British imperialism*. Most Africans, Indians and Coloureds had objected to the Union primarily because only one province, Cape, permitted them to vote. In 1913, the new Union parliament – made up of whites – took away large areas of land owned or occupied by Africans. The seeds of apartheid were already being sown.

In 1924 Hertzog, the leader of the National Party, became Prime Minister, but in 1934 a split occurred in the party over the question of a possible coalition with Smuts' South African Party. This split resulted in the birth of the Gesuiwerde (Purified) National Party under a former church minister and newspaper editor, D. F. Malan.

The new National Party was, its critics say, unduly influenced by Nazi Germany. Certainly Hendrik Verwoerd, who became the Party leader some years later,

Churchman turned politician: Dr D.F. Malan became Prime Minister when the National Party won the 1948 election.

was found by a court to have made the newspaper that he edited 'a tool of the Nazis'. Another man who later also became Prime Minister, B. J. Vorster, was interned during World War II for membership of an organisation regarded as pro-Nazi. Malan declared that South Africa should stay neutral during the war with Germany. The Party's links with Germany are still remembered today in much of the language used by bodies like the ANC which often refer to the South African government as 'fascist'*.

Malan tried to gather as many Afrikaners as possible into the National Party. The 1930s were the years of the Depression* and many Afrikaners were living in poverty in the cities, displaced from their farms. Malan found strong support among these poor whites and the Party continued to cosset them when it gained power. Its policy of apartheid and appeal to Afrikaner nationalism brought victory in the 1948 elections, and it is this party which still rules South Africa today.

Thirty years after the National Party's election win, Biko's Black Consciousness was to be likened to this revival of Afrikaner nationalism.

4
AN ACT OF DEFIANCE

❪ I would like to see groups like ANC, PAC and the Black Consciousness movement deciding to form one liberation group ... ❫

Steve Biko, 1977

The Black Consciousness movement did not emerge from a vacuum. It was, in the words of Barney Pityana, 'self-consciously part of a long line of people's resistance ... a continuation of the tradition of resistance established by the ANC or PAC.'

The organisation that became the ANC was established on 8 January 1912 in Bloemfontein, capital of the Orange Free State and judicial capital of the new Union of South Africa. The ANC was not the first African political association. There had been local groups before, which were usually concerned with specific issues in a township or region. They were followed by the South African Native Convention which met in 1909. Its aim was to extend the non-racial franchise that had existed for more than fifty years in the Cape to the other colonies which were forming the Union.

The Cape liberal tradition was an important one: by the late 1880s, there were 12,000 Africans on the Cape voters' roll and in five Eastern Cape constituencies they made up nearly half the electorate. By the early 1900s about 16% of the voters were black: 10% Coloured and

6% African. Some people, including Africans, believed that they could advance the Africans' political interests by using their vote to elect MPs (Members of Parliament) who would be sympathetic to their cause. The Cape tradition – a practical example of a non-racial principle made into law – came to be idealised and it influenced black political leaders, including those in the ANC, for years.

But Cape liberalism did not extend to the rest of the country. Transvaal, Orange Free State and Natal delegates to the National Convention that set up the Union refused to consider it. Britain, as the colonial power which had a right of veto over the new constitution, would not intervene. Blacks were deprived of their (unsubstantiated) right to be elected to parliament. Further, the constitution provided for the removal of black voters from the Cape common roll by a two-thirds majority of both Houses of Parliament at a joint sitting. It was an ominous constitutional clause in a climate that favoured blacks even less than before.

By the time delegates gathered at the Bloemfontein ANC meeting, there were other indications that all was not well. In terms of a new law, Africans who broke labour contracts committed an offence. This meant that, for example, a farm worker could be sentenced to a fine or a term in jail if he decided conditions were intolerable and he preferred not to work out the term of his contract. For the first time Africans were legally prevented from doing skilled work on the mines. (This was later called 'job reservation' and for years a number of skilled occupations were 'reserved' for whites.) In addition, the Natives' Land Bill was drafted. When it was passed in 1913 it prohibited Africans from owning land in many rural areas outside the 'reserves' – what today are called the homelands. Hundreds of thousands of people were forced from their homes by the Act.

The Bloemfontein delegates decided to act as a pressure group for African advancement and against racial laws. They hoped to achieve better conditions through 'peaceful propaganda', through the election of members to parliament and town and provincial councils of people broadly sympathetic to their beliefs, through protests and inquiries, and ultimately through 'passive action or continued movement'. This last tactic was a clear reference to those practised by Mahatma Gandhi* – including the burning of passes – from the 1890s onwards among the Indians of South Africa in protest against racist laws. He later developed them to bring about independence for India.

For years the ANC leadership consisted mainly of middle class professionals who did not aim for a mass membership, believing that an articulate elite could argue on behalf of the majority of people. They maintained that all people shared South Africa, that the races depended on each other economically, and that the Christian tradition called for the brotherhood of man – not for segregation and discrimination.

But most white voters supported parties that thought otherwise. In 1936, only a handful of MPs opposed a Bill depriving African voters in the Cape of the right to vote on the same electoral roll as whites. In its place they were offered more land in the 'reserves' – although it is still only about 13% of South Africa's total land area – and a different form of political representation. They would be able to vote for white MPs – three in the House of Assembly and four in the Senate. The 'toy telephone' Native Representative Council was set up as an advisory body.

The ANC and other black organisations strongly opposed laws such as these. They also took up 'bread-and-butter' issues that affected people every day, like the pass laws and welfare services. Groups were formed such as the Industrial and Commercial Workers' Union which had a large but short-lived membership. Joint councils between small groups of white liberals and Africans were formed to discuss and oppose the colour bar. The tiny South African Communist* Party had some, but limited, influence on the ANC. (The Communist Party was banned in 1950 and the South African government today

Comrades in struggle: Oliver Tambo (left) and Nelson Mandela who emerged as new-style leaders of the ANC in the 1940s.

accuses it of controlling the ANC. The ANC denies this.)

From 1940, the ANC began to develop mass support and organisation. Under the leadership of Dr A. B. Xuma, it also sharpened its policies, calling for one man, one vote; abolition of the pass laws (some of which began in the 1760s); recognition of African trade unions and an end to the colour bar in industry, as well as more money for health and education. In the early 1940s, a group called the Youth League emerged among the younger members of the ANC. Three of its leaders would later become famous: Nelson Mandela, Walter Sisulu and Oliver Tambo. Its leading light was Anton Lembede. Many of the ideas he put forward, like rejecting foreign leadership and freeing Africans from the psychological shackles of oppression, were echoed by Pan-Africanist Congress leader, Robert Sobukwe, in the late 1950s, and then by Steve Biko in the late 1960s.

The emergence of a more organised, tougher ANC coincided with the rise of Afrikaner nationalism that led Dr Malan to win the 1948 election. Harsher action against blacks through the introduction of apartheid led to the ANC's Defiance Campaign of 1952 – just as whites were celebrating the 300th anniversary of the landing of the Dutch at the Cape. The Campaign marked a change in the way blacks would call for equality: no longer by pleading to the whites but by confrontation through passive resistance.

In the Defiance Campaign, volunteers offered themselves for arrest in protest against racist laws. In many cases they did this by throwing away their passes or by entering the 'whites only' areas of railway stations. Within a few months, more than 8500 people, including some whites, Coloureds, and Indians, had been arrested. Membership of the ANC rocketed in support. The

Defiance Campaign: Africans protest against 300 years of white rule.

government's reply was to 'ban' 52 ANC leaders.

The banning of individuals is a form of punishment peculiar to South Africa. The decision to ban a person is taken by a cabinet minister. No court is involved. There is no right of appeal and the ban usually lasts for two or five years. It can be imposed again after it expires. Usually a ban means that a person is prevented from:

1 Attending 'any gathering, or any particular gathering, or any gathering of a particular nature, at any time, or during any period, or on any day, or during specified times or periods.' This means that a banned person cannot meet more than one individual at a time.

2 Setting foot on any school, university or college ground, any harbour, airport, newspaper or publisher's office.

3 Leaving the magisterial district (a specific area of a town or city) to which he or she has been confined by the minister.
4 Writing anything for publication.
5 Being quoted by any newspaper, magazine, radio, television, or in books.
6 Having any contact with another banned person.

In addition, a banning order often requires the person to:

a) Report regularly, usually once a week, to the police.
b) Resign from any public body or organisation specified by the minister.
c) Remain at home at specified times: usually from 6 pm to 6 am every week day and from 6 pm on Friday to 6 am the following Monday (known as house arrest).

The government also passed laws that made protests against apartheid more difficult and punishable, in some cases, by whipping.

In June 1955, a 'Congress of the People' was held at Kliptown organised by leading anti-apartheid movements. The Congress Alliance drew up a 'Freedom Charter' which set out the essential principles in the struggle for a democratic society in South Africa. It argued for equal treatment of all people before the law; one man, one vote; and the wealth of the country to be better shared among all people rather than concentrated in white hands. The following year, 156 African, Coloured, Indian, and white opponents of apartheid were arrested and charged with high treason. If found guilty they could be hanged. Many were leaders of groups within the Alliance – including the ANC, the Indian Congress, the Coloured People's Organisation and the

On trial: the 156 people charged with treason in the mid-1950s.

TREASON TRIAL

'We the people of South Africa declare for all our country and the world to know: that South Africa belongs to all who live in it, black and white . . .'
The Freedom Charter

(white) Congress of Democrats. One of the accusations against the Treason Trialists concerned the Freedom Charter. The trial took five years to complete: not a single one of the 156 was found guilty. The Freedom Charter is still the main platform for the ANC and a number of other organisations fighting apartheid within South Africa today.

In 1958, however, the ANC split. The new group

Robert Sobukwe: revered by Black Consciousness supporters.

became the Pan-Africanist Congress under Robert Sobukwe. One reason for the split was that the Africanists, as PAC members were called, were suspicious of alliances with non-Africans and especially communists. Many regarded the PAC as anti-white racists, although Sobukwe said that after liberation 'everybody who owed his loyalty to Africa' – even whites – would be regarded as African. The PAC thought, too, that it could prompt a mass uprising which would end apartheid. There were also other differences on strategy with the mainstream ANC leadership.

Sobukwe was a 'revered' figure for many Black Consciousness leaders and Biko met him at least once. With some important differences but also with some similarities, many of the ideas put forward in the late 1950s were to resurface in the philosophy of Black Consciousness a decade later.

5
'POPULAR RAGE'

❝ In the 1960s the African National Congress and the Pan-Africanist Congress had been banned, so the main realities we were confronted with were the power of the police and the leftist noises of the white liberals... ❞

Steve Biko, July 1977

In 1960, both the ANC and PAC called for pass law demonstrations. The pass laws forced Africans to carry a document 'proving' that they had permission to live in a particular city. If the pass was incorrect or if the individual had forgotten to carry it, he or she could be jailed or 'endorsed out' of the district. This often meant being sent to a remote rural area which the government had decided was the individual's homeland, even though he or she may never have seen it before.

The PAC hoped that, in the words of South African historian, Tom Lodge, 'popular rage would cohere into revolutionary uprising'. They decided on a plan of action which involved PAC members, on a set day, leaving their passes at home and presenting themselves at police stations for arrest. The prisons would fill up as more people took part. Industry and commerce would be paralysed by a country-wide general strike that would go on for as long as necessary. It was hoped that these pressures would force the government to abolish passes.

Burning passes: one way of protesting against apartheid laws in 1960.

This would be followed by a 'never-ending stream of campaigns'. The climax would be a struggle for political 'independence' to be concluded by 1963.

Events, however, took a different course. The PAC set 21 March as the day to court arrest, emphasising that the protest should be non-violent. In the African township of Sharpeville near Johannesburg, about 5000 people gathered outside the police station. Behind the wire fence surrounding the station were 300 police called in as reinforcements. Somehow, a scuffle broke out, the fence was holed, a police officer was pushed over, and the crowd surged forward. The police claimed that stones

Sharpeville shootings: some of the dead and injured, shot by police. ▶

were thrown at them. At that stage, police opened fire. Sixty-nine Africans were killed and 180 wounded. Most had been shot in the back.

On the same day, three people were killed in disturbances in the African township of Langa. On 26 March the pass laws were suspended temporarily. A day of mourning for those killed at Sharpeville and Langa was called for 28 March by the president of the ANC, Chief Albert Luthuli. On that day, only a week after the Sharpeville massacre, legislation was introduced to ban the ANC and PAC. The stayaway from work on the day of mourning was largely successful in most big cities, while in Cape Town it continued for a week afterwards. Dramatically, on 30 March, only hours after a state of emergency had been declared, about 30,000 Africans marched peaceably from the townships into the centre of Cape Town to demand the release of their leaders detained under the emergency regulations. The leader of the march, a young PAC member, Philip Kgosana, asked the crowd to disperse on the promise of an interview with the Minister of Justice. The crowd did disperse; Kgosana returned for his appointment and was arrested instead.

It was Sharpeville that really made people throughout the world sit up and take notice of apartheid. There were calls for trade with South Africa to be banned. These are still being voiced today, and some governments have ceased trading with South Africa. Demonstrations against apartheid were held in major cities worldwide, governments were urged to denounce the system. The United Nations publicly condemned it.

Within South Africa, white people had also been shocked by the events at Sharpeville. Many feared reprisals. Nearly R250 million (approximately £125 million) of capital left South Africa; and gold and foreign

Guerrilla war: members of the ANC's armed wing are trained in the bush for the struggle against apartheid.

reserves fell by more than half. Later in 1960 whites voted for a government that would be headed by a president, not a governor-general acting as a representative of the British crown. The following year the country left the Commonwealth*. Afrikaners generally regarded both as a victory; most English-speakers did not as they had a strong loyalty to Britain and the monarchy. Blacks, as usual, were not consulted.

In the aftermath of Sharpeville, both the ANC and PAC formed groups that would encourage political change by armed means. Umkhonto we Sizwe (Spear of the Nation) was the ANC's wing and Poqo (meaning

Rural poverty: part of the Ciskei where Steve Biko grew up.

'alone' or 'pure') the PAC's wing. In the early 1960s both started sabotage campaigns. Both groups were, however, made less of a threat to white South Africa by increased police powers of detention, the use of police spies, and heavy sentences for those found guilty. The High Command of Umkhonto, including Mandela and Sisulu, was arrested and sentenced to life imprisonment in 1964. Sobukwe was jailed as well. The government was so afraid of Sobukwe that after his sentence expired, a special section of a 1963 law, known as the Sobukwe clause, was used to keep him on Robben Island prison for another six years. He was then banned and confined to Kimberley.

Meanwhile, the government had decided, again without consultation, that Africans should find their political place in the sun in Bantustans (homelands). They argued that every African belonged to a tribe which would be given one of ten homelands. (Some did not yet exist, but in time they were all created.) Each homeland would be given self-government with whites training Africans on how to run the state. Soon, the government said, most Africans would stop moving to the 'white' cities and go back to the homelands. One day, when all the homelands had become independent, there would be no more African South Africans, because all would be citizens of a homeland. Africans might come to white areas to work, but there would be no need to give them political rights there.

Hendrik Verwoerd: selling the homeland policy to the Party faithful.

It was a neat theory, polished by the then-Prime Minister, Hendrik Verwoerd. But most blacks saw through the government's arguments. Biko wrote, 'Geographically, ie in terms of land distribution, Bantustans present a gigantic fraud that can find no moral support from any quarters. We find that 20% of the population are in control of 87% of the land while 80% 'control' only 13 per cent.'

Between 1960 and 1983 more than 3.5 million people were moved as apartheid policies were implemented. Nearly all were Africans. Many were dumped in barren rural areas with few facilities and often no places where work could be found. Biko wrote, 'These tribal cocoons called "homelands" are nothing else but sophisticated concentration camps where black people are allowed to "suffer peacefully".'

6
THE BIRTH OF BLACK CONSCIOUSNESS

❛ The biggest mistake the black world ever made was to assume that whoever opposed apartheid was an ally ... ❜

Steve Biko, January 1971

When Biko started medical studies at the University of Natal in 1966, he was committed to the ideal of non-racialism 'almost like a religion'. He became active in the National Union of South African Students (NUSAS), at that time probably the largest non-racial organisation in the country. It represented students at the four 'white' English-language universities and some of the 'tribal colleges' for blacks. NUSAS combined the functions of a trade union for students with a high political profile in opposition to the government. Because of the racial make-up of universities, and the fact that the tightly-controlled 'tribal colleges' usually refused students the right to join NUSAS, blacks were vastly outnumbered: about 27,000 whites to only 3000 blacks. Few were elected to the leadership, although a Coloured was vice-president in the early 1960s.

As Biko became interested in NUSAS, he began to debate with other black students who were critical of whites' attachment to non-racialism. They felt, he later said, that 'whites in general are satisfied with the status quo and are not going to assist completely in moving

away from this situation to one of non-racialism.'
NUSAS was sometimes hypocritical despite its professed
belief in non-racialism. Parties would sometimes be held
in university residences which were barred to blacks. It
was in these debates that Biko began to form his ideas
about Black Consciousness. He was later to write, 'Black
Consciousness is in essence the realisation by the black
man of the need to rally together with his brothers
around the cause of their operation – the blackness of
their skin – and to operate as a group in order to rid
themselves of the shackles that bind them to perpetual
servitude.'

The 1967 NUSAS congress held at Rhodes University
in Grahamstown was the turning point for Biko and
many blacks. Students had been given to understand that,
for the first time at a NUSAS congress, the residences
would be completely integrated. The delegation from the
University of Natal's black section (UNB) decided that if
this did not happen, it would protest, withdraw from the
congress and go home. When the students arrived, they
found the residences were not integrated and that Africans were to sleep in a church. A furious debate followed.
The NUSAS executive brought forward a motion con-
demning the Rhodes authorities for not allowing blacks
in residences. Biko countered with a motion that the
congress should adjourn until an integrated venue could
be found. The whites, he said, 'tended to take us for
granted and . . . could not see why we should not consider
staying in that church.' The congress eventually called for
the abolition of racial segregation on campuses and
Biko's motion was lost.

NUSAS' problem, in the eyes of a former vice-
president, Clive Nettleton, was that 'while preaching the
ideal of non-racialism, the members . . . are unable to live

out their ideals.' White and black 'live in different worlds'. Blacks who normally had no representation had a voice in NUSAS but 'find themselves numerically in a minority and once again without power'. They felt also 'in a forum such as a NUSAS congress that they are representing not only the black students but all black people.'

The divisions in NUSAS that were to lead to the formation of the Black Consciousness movement, and the young Biko's emergence as a major political figure, saddened many people inside and outside student politics. However, the quality of Biko's personality transcended political differences. A friend of Biko's, Father Aelred Stubbs, said, '... despite having precipitated the break with NUSAS ... Steve insisted upon maintaining personal friendships. He was always too big a man to put ideology before persons.'

The idea of a black-only student organisation was first discussed a few days after the Rhodes NUSAS congress. The occasion was a conference of the newly-formed University Christian Movement (UCM). But nothing was done formally about a new student grouping. The following year, 1968, there were sit-ins and protests at several universities. But the NUSAS congress in July, Biko said, swung to the right (partly in the face of increased government threats). 'The overriding impression was that blacks were there in name only [and] the executive that was elected was all white.'

Shortly after the NUSAS congress in July 1968, another UCM conference was held in a small country town called Stutterheim. An issue came up that dramatised both apartheid law and the different attitudes of black and white. Under the Native Laws Amendment Act of 1952, any African born in South Africa was

Biko addresses a SASO meeting in July 1971.

entitled to visit an urban area for up to 72 hours only without requiring a special permit. But the visitor, if required, would have to prove that they had not been in the area for longer than 72 hours.

Some students, Biko later said, felt that they should not observe the law in protest. Others said they should observe it by walking just over the boundaries of the town and returning for another 72 hours. Biko thought this would be hypocritical. He thought that African students should allow themselves to be arrested. White students who were not subject to the law and who would therefore not be arrested should protest. After more debate, the African students demanded and won time to meet alone as a group because they were the ones affected by the law. Once together, they discussed formally the idea of forming a black organisation. It was the beginning of the Black Consciousness movement.

They decided to work towards a conference of black students to be held in December 1968. As they were not representative of their student councils, a convenor from each campus was appointed to tell students what had emerged. In December a conference of Students' Representative Councils from the black campuses decided overwhelmingly in favour of a black organisation. In July 1969 at the University of the North (commonly called Turfloop) the South African Students' Organisation (SASO) was formally founded.

The beginnings were cautious. One reservation, in the words of a communiqué released after the conference, was that 'any move that tends to divide the student population into separate laagers [camps] on the basis of colour is in a way a tacit submission to defeat and seems apparently in agreement with apartheid.' Further, 'in a racially sensitive country like ours, provision for racially exclusive bodies tends to build up resentment and to widen the gap that exists between the races, and the student community should resist all attempts to fall into this temptation.'

But, Biko later wrote, the argument to go ahead was much stronger. 'While . . . we would reject separation in a normal society . . . ours is far from a normal society.' As the SASO communiqué said: 'In choosing to meet on a limited scale rather than not meeting at all, the non-white students shall be choosing the lesser evil, and striving to offset some of the evils that have accrued from the same evil system that made it impossible for them to meet freely with other students.'

The black students' break with NUSAS came, in the eyes of white liberals, at an unfortunate time. NUSAS had been under strong government attack: its president, Ian Robertson, had been banned in 1966 for inviting Senator

Robert Kennedy to South Africa; one of Robertson's successors was forced to leave South Africa permanently to further his studies; another was deported to Britain; and NUSAS had received frequent warnings by government spokesmen that it was 'playing with fire'. In addition, in 1968 the government tried to outlaw all racially mixed organisations that had political views. This would have included NUSAS. There was such a public outcry, shared by some Nationalist supporters, that the bill was changed. But the Prohibition of Political Interference Act was substituted. This made it illegal for anybody to belong to a multiracial political party. The Liberal Party, which wanted one man, one vote for all people, dissolved itself rather than abandon its principles. The Progressive Party, which was more cautiously against apartheid, decided to shed its black membership under protest and to continue in existence. To many white liberals, it seemed as if not only was the government determined to introduce political apartheid but that some blacks were also pursuing racist policies.

SASO aimed to represent 'non-white' students, to establish a solid identity and to make them 'accepted on their own terms as an integral part of the South African community.' But, in the early days, it still accepted NUSAS as the true national union of students. This was partly because the SASO leadership did not want to frighten off mass student support by moving too quickly in promoting Black Consciousness. Biko was elected first president of SASO and spent some time travelling to the different black campuses to build up support.

Father Aelred Stubbs spoke of Biko's 'extraordinary magnetism' at this time. 'His hold on his all-black audiences was almost frightening; it was as if they were listening to a new messiah. Yet the organisation [SASO]

B.J. Vorster: Minister of Justice
who harassed NUSAS leaders.

was not only democratic but from the outset set its face against a leadership cult.'

By the time of the 1970 SASO general students' conference, SASO was much more confident. The term 'non-white' was no longer to be used. 'Black' was the preferred word. Recognition of NUSAS as the national union was withdrawn. The rightwing Afrikaanse Studentebond* was called 'an incorrigible group with whom only nominal contact may be maintained.' For its part, NUSAS was ambivalent towards SASO. It recognised that SASO was better able to represent black students than itself, but many hoped that the split would be short-lived.

One of SASO's most immediate problems was to get permission to organise in the tightly-controlled 'tribal colleges'. The white authorities there were faced with a dilemma. They opposed NUSAS because it was non-racial. They had tried to persuade blacks to form their own separate organisation. Now there was such a body – but it appeared to be becoming a 'black power' organisation. In early 1971 the University of the North agreed to the formation of a SASO branch. After that SASO's task became easier elsewhere. It was not long before wider Black Consciousness movements were established.

7
THE BLACK PEOPLE'S CONVENTION

❝ While the Black People's Convention is non-violent, it should not be forgotten that we are part of a movement which will be confronted with new situations that may require different strategies ... ❞

Steve Biko, July 1977

SASO took the initiative that led to the formation of the most important black political body since the banning of the ANC and PAC. It was called the Black People's Convention (BPC). Biko was careful to point out that the BPC was not trying to compete with the ANC and PAC: 'There will be one movement of revolt against the system of injustice.'

SASO's first step had been to resolve that 'a political movement be formed that shall consolidate the different sections of the black community with an aim towards forming a power bloc.' In early 1971 a SASO executive delegation – among them Biko, Pityana, and Aubrey Mokoape – approached other organisations about the idea of a new movement. Several meetings were held and it was decided that the Interdenominational African Ministers' Association of South Africa (IDAMASA) should chair the negotiations. This grouped many clerics in a discussion body and did not have a reputation for any kind of radicalism.

The conference at Pietermaritzburg in August 1971 was attended by about twenty-six different African organisations. Among those who spoke were Biko and Chief Gatsha Buthelezi, Chief Minister of the KwaZulu homeland. Buthelezi denied the need for a new grouping. He believed that considered support for 'well-motivated people within the separate development policy' – notably

Gatsha Buthelezi: he denied the need for a new black political force.

himself and Curnick Ndamse, a former Fort Hare lecturer who had entered the Transkei cabinet – was needed. They believed that they could achieve most for their people by working through the homelands.

The Pietermaritzburg conference decided to set up a confederate* body to promote African educational, economic, political, and ecumenical development. Biko was part of a committee formed to draft a paper, suggesting ways in which a confederate body could be started. The committee split into two camps: people who wanted to stick to the idea of a co-ordinating body and those – like Biko – who wanted to form a political movement based on the philosophy of Black Consciousness.

In December 1971, a meeting was held by SASO in Soweto near Johannesburg to discuss the purpose of the body. Delegates' opinion was as divided as the committee's. After much debate, it was decided that a new black political body was needed. It would, said Biko, 'focus attention on real issues and ... evolve a method of response from the people to political problems.' Another committee was then formed, partly at Biko's suggestion, to canvass the support of Indians and Coloureds.

By this time, the differences with homeland leaders like Chief Buthelezi were clear. Drake Koka, a trade unionist and former member of the Liberal Party, who was chosen as convenor of a committee to draft a constitution, said the new body would not co-operate with any political institution that had been established by the government. This ruled out any association with homeland leaders or those Indians and Coloureds working within their separate representative councils. That decision, which became a constant theme of Black Consciousness political thinking, gave the movement some of its reputation for exclusivity. The movement argued, however, that people

BPC emerges: Mamphela Ramphele speaks at a congress of the new group.

working within apartheid institutions could not represent black people and were contaminated by their association with apartheid.

In July 1972 the BPC was formed. A three-day congress was held at Edendale near Pietermaritzburg attended by more than one hundred African, Indian and Coloured delegates from around the country. The BPC

wanted to unite blacks 'with a view to liberating and emancipating them from both psychological and physical oppression' and 'to preach, popularise and implement the philosophy of Black Consciousness and black solidarity.' Further, it would try to create a society which was based on social, judicial and economic equality. The BPC planned to mount a recruitment drive which, it hoped, would achieve a membership of one million people by 1975.

What was the reasoning behind the formation of the BPC? It was necessary that a political organisation should exist whose membership was not confined to students, and which would promote black identity and consciousness.

In December 1972 BPC held its first national congress at Hammanskraal near Pretoria. The first national president was elected: Mrs Winnifred Kgware, who had been an active supporter of the formation of a political organisation. Over two hundred delegates attended and BPC's policies began to develop. Opposition was expressed to the South African government's 'dialogue' with other countries. This was a time when the Prime Minister, B. J. Vorster, was trying to develop an 'outward-looking policy', particularly in Africa, with the aim of neutralising opposition to the Pretoria government.

In the same year, the Black Community Programmes (BCP) were formed. BCP's purpose was to set up projects which would benefit the black community. These involved community development projects – clinics and churches, for example. Then there were home industries, mainly in rural areas but sometimes in urban areas too. These cottage industries gave both employment and technical training. The third aspect was leadership training which included skills for women, training for black ministers in the decision-making process of their churches, and youth programmes.

BCP's first director was Bennie Khoapa, a social worker and supporter of Black Consciousness. Biko was among those who soon joined BCP as staff workers. BCP was initially funded by the Christian Institute and the South African Council of Churches. At first there was no structural link with the Black People's Convention but the Black Community Programmes soon fell under the

Black Consciousness umbrella.

When Biko was asked in 1976 why the BCP had been started, he replied: 'The black man is a defeated being who finds it very difficult to lift himself up by his bootstrings. He is alienated — alienated from himself, from his friends, and from society in general. He is made to live all the time concerned with matters of existence: "What shall I eat tomorrow?" We felt that we must attempt to defeat and break this kind of attitude and to instill once more a sense of human dignity within the black man. So what we did was to design various types of programmes, present these to the black community with an obvious illustration that these are done by black people for the sole purpose of uplifting the black community.'

8
BIKO BANNED

6 The liberals criticised us and the conservatives supported us. But this did not last very long. It took the government four years to take measures against us .... It banned individual leaders of the BPC. 9

Steve Biko, July 1977

In 1973, Biko was among those banned under the Suppression of Communism Act of 1950. It did not mean that he was a communist. The then Minister of Justice admitted in 1966 that 'you don't have to be a communist to be banned under the ... Act.' If the Minister considered that the individual was furthering the aims of communism, then that was sufficient grounds for imposing a ban. Several members of the old Liberal Party, which was strongly anti-communist, had been banned in the 1950s and 1960s. Also in the 1950s, a number of ANC leaders had been served with banning orders, effectively curtailing their political activities.

One of the conditions of Biko's banning order was that he had to leave Durban, where he had been working for BCP since August 1972. Earlier in the year, he had abandoned his medical studies and left university to concentrate on political activities. When he returned to King William's Town as a banned person, Father Aelred Stubbs later wrote:

'... it must have seemed that he was returning to his

home town as a failure. He was not qualified for any profession; he had a wife [Ntsiki] and child to support; the chances of employment for a banned "Bantu male" in a "dorp" [small town] like King, with the Security Police everywhere, were slender indeed. But more than that, he would seem to the local community to have failed in every respect. He had not qualified as a doctor, which would have been a great honour for the Ginsberg community [the African township where he and his family lived] and a special pride to his mother, who had sweated for his education.'

However, the period from his banning to his death in 1977 was the most productive time of his life. He gained international recognition as a political figure. He helped establish Zanempilo clinic as a practical example of what Black Community Programmes could do. The clinic was, perhaps, the showpiece of BCP. It had a maternity ward, operating theatre and facilities for teaching nutrition to thousands of Africans in the area outside King William's Town. In addition, Biko helped to set up the Zimele Trust Fund to aid the families of political prisoners.

Biko was not the only one to be banned in early 1973. At the end of February, a parliamentary commission, dominated by government members, reported on an inquiry it had conducted into NUSAS, UCM, the Christian Institute and the Institute of Race Relations. Many people felt that the commission was appointed to provide the government with an excuse to act against some of these organisations. The commission named eight NUSAS leaders whose continued activities in student politics were considered to be 'extremely undesirable'. The commission said that they opposed not only

Black health: over-crowded hospitals are common in South Africa. ▶

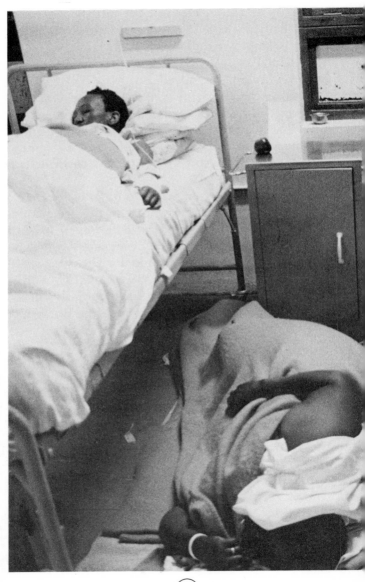

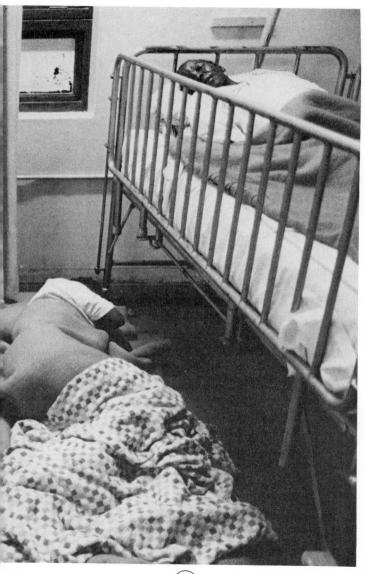

the present government but also the entire existing order including the capitalist system, existing 'moral norms' and forms of authority. They even rejected liberalism. What is more, all the top leaders of NUSAS except one lived in two 'communes'. The eight were promptly banned.

Less than a week later it was the turn of SASO and the BPC. Eight leaders were banned: Biko and Pityana (both former SASO presidents), Jerome Modisane (the current SASO president), Saths Cooper, Drake Koka, B. J. Mafuna, Strini Moodley and Harry Nengwekhulu. Other BPC members were later banned, including Chris Madibeng Mokoditoa (vice-president), Mosebudi Mangena (national organiser), Sipho Buthelezi (secretary-general) and a young poet, Mathe Diseko of the South African Students' Movement (a Black Consciousness movement for school pupils).

These bannings prompted an angry response from some politicians. Mrs Helen Suzman, the anti-apartheid Progressive Party MP, warned that the government had spawned an indestructible black nationalism which was a by-product of white nationalism. 'These drastic bannings will only serve to provoke greater hatred and hostility against the white establishment,' she said. Asked why the student leaders had not been charged in court, the Minister of Justice replied that they did not want to provide the accused with 'a platform' on which to air their beliefs.

It was not long before the newly-elected SASO president, Henry Isaacs, and another seven members who took over offices of the banned eight were also served with banning orders. Nearly all were prohibited from taking any part in the activities of SASO or BPC. Later that year the government revealed that a total of 29 whites and 171 blacks had been served with banning

Helen Suzman: 'bannings will provoke greater hatred', she warned.

orders. In addition, SASO was banned from the university campuses at Fort Hare, the North, and the Western Cape and from areas controlled by the self-governing homeland of Bophuthatswana (indicating that the Black Consciousness movement was worrying the homelands, too).

Biko once described bannings as 'a way of punishing people the state cannot punish under normal law. . . . Many of the banning restrictions are simply designed to inconvenience or exasperate. At first it doesn't seem too inconvenient to have to report to a police station once a week – but after a year it seems an intolerable inconvenience. Talking to one person at a time is designed to inconvenience you by making you repeat everything you said to the last person to the next person as well.

'It is to keep you looking over your shoulder, even in your own home. It is to maintain that kind of tension. Besides, all these provisions are designed to make one commit technical crimes – by breaking the ban. They couldn't make you a criminal before, so they set up artificial provisions, and if you are caught contravening these you are technically a criminal.'

His banning order was meant to be the end of his political career. It was not. In the words of a friend, Dr Trudi Thomas: 'He hobnobbed with the great and the influential who sought him out in his banishment, which rather neatly turned his intended Siberia into a Mecca.' As the years of his banning went on, an increasing stream of diplomats, foreign correspondents, academics and politicians went to King William's Town to meet Biko. This was partly a reflection of the growing strength of the Black Consciousness movement, and it was partly Biko's own reputation.

Biko's reputation had increased, too, as a result of the evidence he gave over five days at the SASO/BPC trial in May 1976. Nine leaders from these organisations were charged with a variety of offences including 'endangering the maintenance of law and order', conspiring to 'transform the state by unconstitutional, revolutionary and/or violent means', to 'create and foster feelings of racial hatred' and to discourage foreign investment. But many believed the whole philosophy of Black Consciousness was really on trial.

It was Biko's first opportunity to be heard in public since his banning more than three years before. (A quirk of the law allowed banned people to be quoted in the press if they were giving evidence in a court.) He needed to tread a careful line between honesty and not drawing the wrath of the court down on his head or those of the accused. To a large extent he succeeded, even under hostile questioning from counsel for the prosecution. The judge, too, showed what many people considered strong bias against the accused – and a simplistic view of the world.

When asked to clarify his (Biko's) statement about 'blacks being subjected by the white government to "direct terrorism"', Biko's reply was blunt. 'I am talking about the violence in which people are baton-charged by police, beaten up .... I am talking about police firing on unarmed people in places like Sharpeville ... I am talking about the kind of situation you get at Dimbaza where there is no food [and] hardly any furniture for people.'

In the end, the defendants were all found guilty. They were sentenced to five or six years imprisonment. It was advance warning that pressure on the Black Consciousness movement would be stepped up.

9
SOWETO

❛ Soweto! The boldness, dedication, sense of purpose, and clarity of analysis of the situation – all of these things are a direct result of Black Consciousness ideas among the youth of Soweto and elsewhere. ❜

Steve Biko, July 1977

In 1976, Soweto was as important and shocking an event as Sharpeville 16 years before. Both were milestones in South African history, showing the depth of black anger at apartheid. Both concentrated world attention on South Africa again, and both led to a large outflow of foreign money from the South African economy, causing a crisis of confidence among sections of the white South African population.

Sharpeville had begun as a protest against the pass laws. The demonstrations at Soweto began as a protest against a government instruction that high school pupils should be taught some subjects in Afrikaans. This was unpopular for several reasons: most African teachers could barely speak Afrikaans; good English was thought to be a necessary qualification for many white-collar jobs; and Afrikaans was regarded as the language of the oppressor.

Dr Andries Treurnicht, Deputy Minister of Bantu Education, was responsible for the ruling. He and his supporters regarded any African advancement in the economy as a threat to their jobs. He was, and is, a politician in the mould of Dr Hendrik Verwoerd, with never a doubt that his policies were right. He justified his ruling on the compulsory use of Afrikaans by saying: 'In the white areas of South Africa, where the government provides the buildings, gives the subsidies and pays the teachers, it is surely our right to determine the language division.' Treurnicht is now leader of the rightwing Conservative Party, a breakaway group from the ruling National Party which it regards as dangerously liberal.

The immediate roots of the Soweto uprising lay among the township's schoolchildren. For years, most people, black and white, saw education for Africans as the key to advancement. African parents would make great personal and financial sacrifices to make sure that their

Soweto protest: 'We are not fighting,' said one of the children's leaders, but dozens were shot dead by police.

children went to school and got a better education than they had, and ultimately a more skilled and better paid job. The South African economy also needed more educated Africans: between 1960 and 1970, the number of Africans in white-collar posts grew by 180 per cent. Black Consciousness began to appeal to this better-educated group.

Black Consciousness also had some influence over the South African Students' Movement (SASM), established three years before, which convened a meeting in the township on 13 June 1976. There the Soweto Students' Representative Council (SSRC) was formed of two pupils from each of the township's schools. Its response to the mounting anger at the forced use of Afrikaans was to call a demonstration in protest.

The sixteenth of June is now remembered, in South Africa and in many other countries, as Soweto Day. On that day 15,000 children planned to march to the Orlando Stadium – one of the few large open spaces in Soweto. Nearly 10,000 children had reached Orlando West Junior Secondary School (closed since the middle of May because pupils had refused to attend classes) when a message reached one of the leaders that the police were coming. He appealed to the crowd to stay calm: 'We are not fighting.'

The police arrived in ten van-loads. They were armed with revolvers, semi-automatic rifles and tear-gas cannisters. No police order was heard telling the crowd to disperse. What happened next is a matter for dispute. A policeman probably threw a tear-gas cannister into the crowd. Children in the front scattered, then re-grouped. More tear-gas was thrown. Pupils began to throw stones at the police. The officer in charge, Colonel Johannes Kleingeld, took out his revolver and fired a shot into the

The first victim: Hector Pieterson's body is carried by a friend.

crowd. Hector Pieterson, aged 13, was killed – the first victim of Soweto. More police opened fire. Colonel Kleingeld used his Sten gun (a small sub-machine gun) because, he said later, it had 'a more demoralising effect than a pistol shot'. A peaceful protest was rapidly turning into a massacre.

The crowd scattered and then came together, gathering more people as news of the shooting spread. Passing cars were stoned – especially white Volkswagen Beetles used by the Bantu Administration Department (BAD). Administration buildings were set on fire. Any symbol of white authority and control became a target for attack. Beerhalls and liquor shops were looted, and two white men were killed.

Unrest continued all day in several parts of Soweto. When residents returned from their day's work in Johannesburg that evening, they were met by police with batons and tear-gas. Stones were thrown at the police: many parents joined the struggle. Horrific stories were told of the police arresting demonstrators, then assaulting and shooting them in the Orlando police station. By the end of the second day the official death toll was fifty-four. However, a Christian Institute leader was told by a black policeman that in one area of Soweto alone they collected 176 corpses. Just under a week after the first deaths, the compulsory use of Afrikaans was suspended.

It was not long before unrest reached other areas: first in another black township, Alexandra, close to Johannesburg's wealthy white northern suburbs. Here a roadblock was built under the banner: 'Why kill kids for Afrikaans?' University campuses reacted in solidarity. In August, Coloureds in Cape Town took the struggle to the city centre – as Soweto students had tried to do in Johannesburg when, protesting against the detention of

Ready, aim, fire: police in action during the Soweto uprising.

many of their leaders, they attempted to march on police headquarters in the 'white' city. They were turned back on the road between Soweto and Johannesburg by police gunfire. Three students were killed.

It was in Cape Town that the conduct of the police was seen first-hand by many whites; previous, well-documented allegations of brutality had usually been denied by the government and ignored by whites. Now, within a few hundred yards of parliament, the police could be seen in action. The death toll continued to mount. In December the *Rand Daily Mail*, a liberal Johannesburg newspaper, carefully documented 499 deaths. The government acknowledged only 386. By the end of 1976, there was scarcely a corner of South Africa that had been left untouched.

Why did Soweto happen? Some of the first official response was to blame 'agitators' and 'communists' – and then Black Consciousness. The Minister of Justice, J. T. Kruger, asked why the students walked with upraised fists. 'Surely this is the sign of the Communist Party?' Colonel Theunis Swanepoel, once chief interrogator of the Special Branch, also spied communism. In what he called a stone-throwing mob of more than 4000, he saw a man in front with arms outstretched and fists clenched. 'It was the sign resembling the horns of an ox, and I noticed the crowd had suddenly closed in on us, approaching in flanks from the left and right.' The ox-horn sign, he went on, was 'a well-known communist tactic'. Kruger, a few days later, said that the riots were 'definitely organised', naming 'black power groups' like SASO and the BPC.

To what extent Black Consciousness influenced the demonstrators of Soweto is a matter of some dispute. Kruger and the government found it a useful whipping post, but more for their own political ends than for any desire to get at the truth. Conjuring up the spectre of 'black power' to frighten white voters was a lot easier than accepting responsibility for the entire range of conditions that sparked off the protests. Much of the evidence by people who were actually there is that the ideas of Black Consciousness had got through to both the African pupils of Soweto and the Coloureds of the Western Cape.

A series of recent events had also given blacks new confidence and many believed the time was ripe for change in South Africa. A wave of strikes in 1972 had been successful; the black liberation movement, Frelimo, had come to power in Mozambique in 1974 after the collapse of the Portuguese empire. Frelimo's victory greatly heartened many blacks, not least because it showed that a southern African liberation movement could succeed. The collapse of the Portuguese empire also deprived white South Africa of the buffer states of Mozambique and Angola: black rule was now much closer and, in time, it would make the infiltration of ANC guerrillas easier.

Further, the South African government was beginning to move towards a kind of negotiated end to the Rhodesia/Zimbabwe problem. Rhodesia (now called Zimbabwe) was a self-governing British colony. It was experiencing major unrest as Rhodesia's whites, under the leadership of Prime Minister Ian Smith, had declared unilateral independence from Britain in 1966 in an attempt to avoid black majority rule being introduced by London. Prime Minister B. J. Vorster had given white Rhodesia invaluable South African help. But opinion, particularly in the United States, was turning towards ending this rebellion, so that black majority rule could be introduced. Mr Vorster wanted Rhodesia off his back — he was flying to meet the US Secretary of State, Henry Kissinger, as Soweto erupted. Black South Africans saw the Pretoria government willing to press white Rhodesia towards accommodation with its blacks: might not the same thing be done in South Africa?

10
'A MISERABLE AND LONELY DEATH'

❝ Listen, if you guys want to do it your way, you
have got to handcuff me and bind my feet together
so that I can't respond.... And I'm afraid you may
have to kill me in the process even if it's not your
intention. ❞

Steve Biko, 1977

The first Black Consciousness leader to die in Special
Branch detention was Mapetla Mohapi. He was detained
for allegedly smuggling three youths into Botswana for
guerrilla training. Transferred to a police cell at Kei
Road, a small village near his home in King William's
Town, he managed to smuggle out a letter to his wife,
Nohle, saying that he was in good spirits.

On 15 August 1976, the Special Branch came to the
Mohapi house to say that Mapetla had committed suicide. They said that he had hanged himself from the bars
in his cell with his jeans. The police produced a suicide
note – but Mohapi's wife and a handwriting expert said
later at the inquest that it was a crude forgery.

The most chilling evidence at the inquest was given by
another Black Consciousness leader, Thenjiwe Mtintso,
a reporter on the liberal newspaper, the *Daily Dispatch*,
who was detained shortly after Mohapi's death. She
demonstrated to the court how a burly Special Branch

officer had made her squat on the floor, gripped her between his knees, wound a towel round her throat and tightened the ends. As he did it, he said: 'Now you can see how Mohapi died.' He repeated this several times, loosening the towel only when she was nearly unconscious.

The lawyer for the Mohapi family argued that all the evidence suggested homicide, probably caused by 'an over-zealous interrogator over-stepping the mark'. The magistrate at the inquest found that nobody was to blame for Mohapi's death. But he stopped short of delivering a formal verdict of suicide.

Soweto and its aftermath marked the beginning of frequent detentions of Black Consciousness leaders. In Port Elizabeth, Barney Pityana and his wife, Dimza, were held regularly; in King William's Town and East London, Biko, Nohle Mohapi, Thenjiwe Mtintso, and others were detained for long periods. Dr Mamphela Ramphele, doctor at the Zanempilo clinic, was banned to the Eastern Transvaal. Biko's banning order had already been tightened, preventing him from working for BCP. SASO and BPC officials in different parts of the country were served with banning orders. Biko was charged with obstructing the course of justice by telling students to lie in court. This accusation was not upheld in court and Biko was acquitted.

Then, on 18 August 1977, Steve Biko was arrested in Grahamstown after having been stopped at a road block. He was travelling with Peter Jones, a BPC organiser. (It later emerged that Biko and Jones were returning from a meeting in Cape Town. This was a contravention of Biko's banning order.) Three weeks later, on 12 September, Biko died in a Pretoria police cell.

The reaction of the Minister of Justice, J. T. Kruger, to

Biko's death was to tell a National Party congress: 'It leaves me cold .... I shall also be sorry if I die.' He went on to imply that Biko had died after a hunger strike. Donald Woods, editor of the *Daily Dispatch* and friend of Biko's, responded to Kruger's statement by saying that he and Biko had a pact: 'If any of four reasons for his death was alleged, I would know it was untrue. One was hunger strike.'

Biko's funeral was held in King William's Town. Thirteen western countries sent diplomats and the ceremony was attended by at least 15,000 people. Thousands of mourners, however, were prevented from attending as police set up road blocks in many areas.

There had been an immediate outcry when the news of Biko's death flashed around the world. He was the forty-sixth person to die since detention without trial was introduced in 1963. In the 18 months before Biko's death, 17 people had died. Why was this death so worthy of attention? It was partly because of Biko's stature, both inside and outside South Africa, and because Black Consciousness was recognised as a major force in South Africa. It was partly the campaigning of Donald Woods and others who had known Biko and who recognised his outstanding abilities. Many were journalists, politicians, lawyers and diplomats who were able to attract widespread attention. And it was partly the nature of evidence reluctantly conceded by the Special Branch under intense questioning from Sydney Kentridge, lawyer for the Biko family, at the inquest.

The full story of what happened to Biko during the weeks he was in detention is known only to the Special Branch. But from the inquest it emerged that he and Jones had been transferred to Port Elizabeth, 80 miles from Grahamstown. Both were detained under the Terrorism

Funeral crowd: Steve Biko's casket is carried before his burial.

Act which barred any communication with people outside. Jones was detained without trial for a staggering 533 days and released only in February 1979. He later wrote a graphic account of his detention in which he describes the gruelling interrogations and brutal beatings that the Special Branch dealt out to try to gain information. The beatings became increasingly violent, and on several occasions Jones was attacked with metal hosepipes.

'Every time I tried to defend my head with my hands the pipes would move to the back, the kidney area, or attack the hands. I found it impossible to cope with all the immense pain and I turned and faced the wall. . . . closing my eyes, hoping for oblivion, which never came, as blows rained down on my head and back.'

At the inquest, the court heard how Biko was held in a cell for 20 days, naked, deprived of exercise (a contravention of regulations), unable to communicate with anybody besides his captors, without books or papers and given inadequate food. He was visited once by a magistrate who did nothing about his complaints.

Then, on the morning of 6 September, Biko was taken to Room 619 of the Special Branch's headquarters in Port Elizabeth. The Special Branch accused him of compiling pamphlets inflaming the people of Port Elizabeth to riot. Major Harold Snyman, second-in-command of the Port Elizabeth Special Branch and head of Biko's interrogation team, said that Biko had denied it when the questioning began at 10.30am; by 6pm he was admitting it.

Kentridge: 'Did you put physical pressure on him?'
Snyman: 'No.'
Kentridge: 'How did you break him down?'
Snyman: 'We told Biko he would remain in detention until he had answered the questions satisfactorily.'

Sydney Kentridge: lawyer for the Biko family at the inquest.

Major Harold Snyman: head of Biko's interrogation team.

Kentridge: 'Biko was detained in 1976 for 101 days. What sort of threat do you think it would be to him to threaten to keep him in detention until he answered questions? What can you do to a man who insists on keeping silent?'

No answer.

Snyman said that at 6pm Biko was allowed to rest until 7am the next day. But this changed under cross-examination.

Kentridge: 'And at 6pm, after your first day of interrogation, you were relieved by Lieutenant Wilken's night squad of three?'

Snyman: 'Correct.'

Kentridge: 'They were the night interrogators, were they?'

Snyman: 'Correct.'

But a few minutes later, Snyman said Wilken's squad 'were only there to guard him while he rested.'

The Special Branch admitted that Biko had been kept shackled hand and foot in the interrogation room.

Kentridge asked Colonel Pieter Goosen, head of the Security Police in Port Elizabeth: 'What right did you have to keep a man in chains for 48 hours?'

Goosen: 'I have the full power to do it. Prisoners could attempt suicide or escape.'

Kentridge: 'Let's have an honest answer — where did you get your powers?'

Goosen: 'It is my power.'

Kentridge: 'Are you people above the law?'

Goosen: 'I have full powers to ensure a man's safety.'

Kentridge: 'I am asking for the statute.'

Goosen: 'We don't work under statutes.'

Kentridge: 'Thank you very much. That is what we have always suspected.'

Colonel Goosen and Lieutenant Wilken: Port Elizabeth security police.

Later the police claimed that at the beginning of the second day of interrogation, Biko was confronted with 'certain facts' about the pamphlets. Snyman said that sworn statements by other detainees implicating Biko were put to him on the morning of 7 September. The sworn statements, once handed into the court, however, were found to date from 15–30 September. Mr Kentridge argued that this was a 'smear prepared after Biko's death'. Other police officers admitted that no documents were put to Biko that morning. Later, in his summing-up, Mr Kentridge was to say that, 'What we have here is a clear and plain case of deliberate perjury on the part of Major Snyman.'

After these 'facts' were put to Biko, Snyman reported in one of his versions of events, 'the detainee was very aggressive, then became beserk, threw a chair at me, and rushed with clenched fists at other members of the staff. After a tremendous struggle he fell with his head against a wall and sustained an injury on his body.' That, the police claimed, was probably how Biko had suffered the injuries which caused his death, although one witness said his injuries could have been self-inflicted.

But this version of events did not satisfy Mr Kentridge. The pathological evidence from the post-mortem showed that the injuries to Biko's brain were suffered beyond reasonable doubt by 7.30am on 7 September. Specialists in brain damage said that Biko would have certainly suffered a period of unconsciousness. Yet this had not been indicated in the evidence or affidavits given by the Special Branch. Other medical evidence revealed that brain damage can cause irrational behaviour – which could explain the 'scuffle' mentioned by Snyman. There were, too, a number of discrepancies in the police evidence about the 'scuffle'.

Mr Kentridge said: 'On the morning of 6 September, Biko went into the interrogation room alive and well. At 7.30am on 7 September he was a physical and mental wreck. It is clear, therefore, that Mr Biko suffered his injuries either while in the custody of the night squad (under Wilken) or the day squad (under Snyman).'

The role of two doctors, called in by the Special Branch, was critical. Dr Ivor Lang, the district surgeon, was summoned by Goosen soon after he had been told that there had been an 'incident' on the morning of 7 September. Lang issued a certificate saying he saw no sign of injuries. Mr Kentridge said that by this stage Biko had been 'smashed up'. The Special Branch wanted a certificate saying he was unhurt so they could deny any assault if Biko went to court. Further, it was probable that Biko had been injured sufficiently to alarm the Special Branch: they just hoped it would not be fatal.

Under cross-examination Dr Lang conceded that his certificate was 'highly inaccurate'. Neither he nor the chief district surgeon, Dr Benjamin Tucker, admitted to noticing many of the injuries that must have been there when – or if – they examined Biko: a cut lip, a bruise near

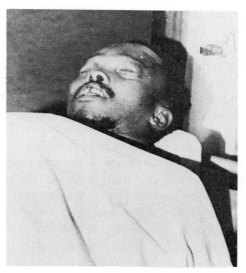

In death: Biko's body after the post-mortem.

his second rib, swollen hands and feet (from the manacles used to chain him) and an abrasion on his forehead. Neither questioned him about the lip or forehead injuries – despite their fears that he may have suffered brain damage.

The only explanation for the behaviour of the doctors is that they did not want to embarrass the Special Branch and that they entered into a conspiracy of silence. They appeared to swallow Goosen's apparent belief that Biko was shamming. This theory justified the police's reluctance to send him to hospital.

The doctors also appeared to continue to believe that Biko was not seriously ill even despite a lumbar puncture that showed possible brain damage and a reflex test that could not be shammed. Dr Tucker agreed that the dying Biko could be transported by road to Pretoria for further tests. Biko was taken naked in the back of a Land Rover, with only security policemen as escorts and a bottle of water as medical equipment, nearly 800 miles to Pretoria prison hospital. When he was delivered, Lieutenant Wilken continued to insist that Biko was shamming. There, Mr Kentridge said, Biko 'died a miserable and lonely death on a mat on a stone floor in a prison cell.'

The inquest lasted for a total of 15 days during which time many instances of lies, inconsistencies, evasions and cover-ups were revealed. Among the points that were not settled was the hunger strike theory put forward by Kruger. Goosen refused to comment on why his minister had implied Biko had died after a hunger strike. The magistrate presiding at the inquest would not allow Kruger to be called to give evidence. He took less than three minutes to deliver his finding: 'The cause or likely cause of Mr Biko's death was a head injury ...[which] was probably sustained on the morning of 7 September during a scuffle with security police in Port Elizabeth. The available evidence does not prove that death was brought about by an act or omission involving an offence by any person.'

11
A POTENT FORCE

❝ Steve as I prefer to remember him: a man full of life, jocular, and yet one who had the ability to express even the deepest thoughts in a light-hearted manner ... He never sought personal glory but served the cause of justice and liberation as part of a dynamic movement ... ❞

Barney Pityana, August 1987

Biko's death in detention shattered most of the people who had known him and deeply affected millions of others. Two of his close friends recall dreaming of him and talking to him on his death. Barney Pityana was in detention in the centre of Port Elizabeth: 'On the night in which he died, I was engaged in a most memorable and animated discussion with Steve. The episode seemed to end with Steve entrusting to me the future and well-being of his children. I remember laughing this off. Maybe it was because I tend not to take seriously my friends' death wishes. But I now know that that was his last will and testament.'

Donald Woods recalls lying awake, questioning a 'mental image of Steve lying dead.... after an hour or so of these intense questions I suddenly received clear answers from an acutely real, clear image of Steve ...

"What happened? Who did it? What does he look like?"

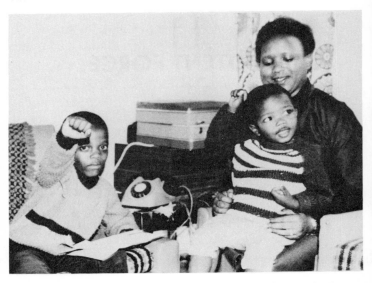

Biko's sister, Bandi, with her brother's two children after his death.

"There were three of them, as a matter of fact. But the main one was a young guy, very strong. But it doesn't matter, really."

'I had the impression from this that he meant it didn't matter in the sense that the blows (certainly more than one blow) directed at him had done more lasting harm to the System than to him.'

Five weeks after his death, on 19 October 1977, the entire range of Black Consciousness organisations in South Africa were banned under the Internal Security Act. Among those declared illegal were SASO, BPC, BCP, SASM, the Black Parents' Association, and the Soweto SRC. Seven whites were banned the same day, including Donald Woods and another close friend of Biko's, the Reverend David Russell, as well as leaders of the Christian Institute which had helped to start BCP.

Government action did not stop at bannings. A total of 47 people were placed in what the Internal Security Act called 'preventive detention' — in effect admitting that the detainee had not committed any offence. Among them was virtually the entire leadership of the Black Consciousness movement. By the end of November at least sixty-five Black Consciousness leaders and organisers were still in detention, not having been charged with any offence. These detainees included Percy Qoboza, editor of the largest-selling black newspaper, *The World*. The paper and its weekend edition were banned as well. The banning of Woods and *The World*, along with Qoboza's detention, marked what many journalists thought was the end of press freedom in South Africa.

The death of Biko and the October 19 crackdown marked, too, what many thought of as the end to any hopes of peaceful change in South Africa. The government, it seemed, had deliberately cut down people and organisations wanting to negotiate with the whites.

Just as there had been in the early 1960s, there followed a period of political quiet among many blacks and whites. A few Black Consciousness groups were re-formed, notably the Azanian* People's Organisation (AZAPO) which today has a much more Marxist approach than any of the banned bodies. Then, in August 1983, the United Democratic Front (UDF) was launched.

The UDF is an umbrella body which now has 700 organisations affiliated to it. Its goal is a united, non-racial, democratic South Africa. Its opponents say it is nothing more than a front for the banned ANC. The UDF has organised a number of protests at government laws. But in February 1988 the UDF, 14 of its affiliates and AZAPO were banned from performing 'any activities or acts whatsoever.' The organisations were not banned as

Banning protest: students demonstrate against the banning of the UDF.

such, as the ANC, PAC and Black Consciousness groups had been: they were simply not allowed to do anything except keep their accounts in order.

This was enforced under state of emergency regulations. An emergency was declared first in July 1985 after a period of widespread unrest and many deaths. The trouble more or less coincided with the introduction of a new constitution for South Africa. This gave Coloureds and Indians – but not Africans – their own chambers of parliament. In terms of numbers of MPs and power, however, the whites still had control. Many Coloureds and Indians rejected the reforms that the State President, P. W. Botha, brought in.

Since late 1984, the mood of South Africans opposed to apartheid has swung a lot. Barney Pityana has described it as 'an amazing oscillation in black politics between militancy and dynamism, opportunism and sheer fatigue, hope and despair.' Sometimes it seems as if the government is rattled; then a new wave of emergency regulations, police action, bannings, detentions and other measures show that the state is a long way from being defeated.

The outside world's approach to apartheid has also oscillated between hope and despair. In the mid-1980s the hope was that comprehensive, mandatory economic sanctions would help to bring apartheid to an end. But these sanctions were never applied. Some more, limited sanctions were implemented. They did not, however, force the government to negotiate with the black majority. This was a great blow to those who had thought that sanctions would bring instant results.

In the mid-1980s, some people interpreted the revival of the ANC both as a diplomatic force in world politics and as a guerilla organisation inside South Africa as a signal that apartheid would soon be overcome. Certainly there was increased confidence among many black South Africans that 'liberation' was near. But the state soon began to use its power again. As the 1990s approached, it seemed unlikely that the apartheid system would be swept away before the turn of the century.

What, then, did Steve Biko and the Black Consciousness movement contribute? Perhaps their most important achievement was a revival of black confidence. Hope and despair still mingle, but nobody now expects black militancy to disappear.

The organisations that Biko helped found, including SASO, BPC, and BCP, no longer exist. Even the remaining Black Consciousness groups are over-shadowed by bodies that follow a non-racial approach rather than the 'blacks only' view Biko once espoused.

But, as Barney Pityana, has pointed out, the Black

Consciousness movement in the 1960s and 1970s did not see itself as a rival or alternative to established organisations; nor did its leaders seek to replace the Mandelas and Sobukwes. Black Consciousness also set itself a limited programme as it struggled to establish itself. What was right then, politically and tactically, is not necessarily right today. Many of the Black Consciousness advocates of the 1960s and 1970s are today in the forefront of organisations that are non-racial in approach.

Biko himself became a symbol of resistance. His name is still a potent force throughout the world. He was undoubtedly one of the most important political figures to emerge in South Africa and will be remembered long after most of the white politicians are forgotten. He and the Black Consciousness movement gave back to blacks, particularly Africans, both pride and hope.

GLOSSARY

Afrikaanse Studentebond Union of Afrikaans-speaking students at South African universities.

Azania The Black Consciousness name for South Africa.

Black Consciousness The movement started by Steve Biko in the 1960s and '70s which aimed to re-establish black self-confidence and worked towards achieving black majority rule.

The Commonwealth An association of states which have been ruled by Great Britain in the past. Official title: 'The Commonwealth of Nations'.

Communism A political theory based on the writings of the 19th century philosopher, Karl Marx, which aims at a society founded on equality and communal ownership.

Confederacy An alliance of different groups.

The Depression A worldwide economic slump in the 1930s which led to mass unemployment.

European Enlightenment An 18th century movement which sought to emphasise the importance of reason, hence this period became known as the 'Age of Reason'.

Fascism An extreme right-wing movement which is nationalistic, authoritarian and undemocratic.

Franchise The right to vote.

Mahatma Gandhi Social reformer and political leader, famous for helping to achieve independence for India through organised passive resistance. He lived in South Africa between 1893–1914 where he actively opposed racial discrimination.

Imperialism The policy of a state to extend its rule over other territories.

Napoleonic Wars These wars occurred between 1804–1815 when the self-proclaimed emperor of France, Napoleon Bonaparte, attempted to extend the French empire. He was defeated by British and Prussian forces at the Battle of Waterloo.

National Party The largest political party in parliament in South Africa which has been in power since 1948 and introduced the system of apartheid.

FURTHER READING LIST

Biko, Steve, *I Write What I Like* (Penguin Books, 1988).
Edited with a personal memoir by Aelred Stubbs and with an
introduction by Barney Pityana. It contains some of Biko's best
writing.
Biko, Steve, *The Testimony of Steve Biko* (Granada, 1978).
Biko's evidence in the SASO/BPC trial, edited by Millard Arnold
with an appendix on the Biko inquest.
Blair, Jon, and Fenton, Norman, *The Biko Inquest* (Rex Collings,
1978).
Strong dramatisation based on the inquest records.
Davenport, T. R. H., *South Africa: A Modern History*
(Macmillan, 1961, second edition).
Authoritative senior school or university history.
Lodge, Tom, *Black Politics in South Africa Since 1945* (Longman,
1983).
Good, very detailed.
Omond, Roger, *The Apartheid Handbook* (Penguin, 1986).
A guide to South Africa's race policies.
Survey of Race Relations (various editions) (SA Institute of Race
Relations).
Essential annual survey of nearly everything that happens in
South Africa.
Woods, Donald, *Biko* (Penguin Books, 1987).
The first and best-known book on Biko's life. The revised and
updated edition has a valuable epilogue by Peter Jones on his
treatment after being arrested with Biko.

INDEX